THE CABINET

SETHIAN GNOSTICISM IN THE POSTMODERN WORLD

MORICARIO

Introduced and edited by
RUNE ØDEGAARD

KRYSTIANIA

The Cabinet: Sethian Gnosticism
in the postmodern world
© Rune Ødegaard 2014

Published by Krystiania
Oslo, Norway

First edition 2014

Cover: Joachim Svela / formbureauet
formbureauet.com

Set with 12/20 pt. Arno Pro
Paper: 70 g Crawford Opaque Colonial White

Krystiania Publishing has a green profile, and strives to publish books of natural, renewable and recyclable materials.
The paper is acid- and lignin-free, made from sustainable forests. Our books are CoC-certified, by either FSC®, SFI® or PEFC™, depending on where they are produced.

ISBN 978-82-93295-09-9

www.krystiania.com

Contents

About this book 6
What is the Moricario 8
Acknowledgments 10
The Moricario 11
The Preparations 12
Preludium 14
The song of Seth 15
The Calling of the Watchers of the Work 17
Retrieving the Tools 21
The Dedication 26
The Epiphany 30
The vision of the Cross 31
The Cloak of Seth 34
Intermezzo 36
The Litany of Adamas 37
The Rite of the Self-born 41
The Blessing of the River 44
The Secret Seal 46
Postludium 47
Veni Sethorai 48
The Work of the Cabinet 50
   Opening the Cabinet 50
   Two Sacraments 53
   Closing the Cabinet 56
Appendix 58
   The Book of Adamas 58
Krystiania publications 81

Call for me and I will be the hidden door at the threshold of time.

"The Book of Zorakatora"

About this book

This is the third and last book of the Sethian trilogy presenting the Gnostic school of *Amarantian Sethianism,* as it is understood and worked in the organization Sodalitas Sanctum Seth (SSS).
As translator and editor of this book, I have been commissioned to render this spiritual current understandable for those who wish to study Sethianism within the SSS or as an individual seeker.
The first book in this trilogy is *The Key: Sethian Gnosticism in the postmodern world*. In that book I describe the essential keys necessary to read the original Sethian scriptures as a living tradition of today.
The second book, *The Gate: Sethian Gnosticism in the postmodern world* is a collection of Sethian material deriving from the holy book of the SSS, namely *The Charaxio*. Having read the Key, the reader may use his or her new knowledge to open the Lock of The Gate.
This third book is called *The Cabinet: Sethian Gnosticism in the postmodern world,* even though the book presented in this volume is *The Moricario*. This book of praxis has occasionally been given to probationers for initiation into the Circle, one of the currents of the SSS.
As a preparatory work, The Moricario reveals to the Sethian initiator whether the seeker is able to gain access to the Cabinet where all Sethian work is performed.
This book is published for study purposes only. As a disclaimer, I do not recommend anyone practice the rituals or material in this book. In the SSS these workings are performed while instructed and guided by a senior member or a master of the tradition. If you choose to practice the ceremonies in this book, you bear sole responsibility.

This text gives a clear view of the sacramental language and setting of this particular branch of Gnosticism.

Rune Ødegaard
Oslo, Norway
February 2014

What is the Moricario

Legends told within the SSS have it that Moricario was one of the aeons within the aeon of Seth, something equal to being one of his sons or daughters. It is possible that Moricario actually is the combination of the feminine and masculine names of an aeon, so that the name actually is Mori and Cario.

The aeon Moricario is described as a stepping stone or a place between the places, the entrance to the room where you are already present, a broken circle or a bridge floating in thin air. It is psychologically equivalent to an experiential shift in perspective, as when focusing on the square or the lines below. However it never appears as lines and a square at the same time. The focus of the mind changes rapidly between the two figures.

X	X	X	X
X	X	X	X
X	X	X	X
X	X	X	X
X	X	X	X
X	X	X	X

Thus entering the realm or fullness of Moricario is to begin a process of mingling your present views, perspectives and memories with what the Gnostic teachers of old understood as the key to the mental cage, gnosis. Thus it is considered a way of tuning the practitioner to the Sethian work of redeeming him or herself from the less fortunate forces of matter and mind. In the end, the seeker may be able to rediscover the fullness that was never actually lost.

Moricario is an aeon and some kind of pathway or transforming device. According to legend this aeon was invited to enter the material world of flesh to become a teacher of humankind. However Moricario approached Seth and asked to be incarnated in a book rather than in a human body. And as it was proposed, so it was done. And Horaia, the spouse of Seth, provided Moricario with his new flesh, a body of ink and paper.

It is said that Moricario was united to the book through music and the sound of a clock or a bell. And as the clock gave its final sound, the work was fulfilled. An eternity was comprised between the pages of a book.

This book was then given to a Sethian monk living as a councilor in the House of Abel, and he was the first to read this book to his children and instruct them in its customs and curiosities.

Another story tell us that the book was empty when opened by the monk, but there was a very dreamy kind of whistling music deriving from the book; almost impossible to hear. And listening to this music the monk gave ink to the word like veins worn by the structure of the book.

Such are the legends of Moricario.

According to the SSS, Moricario comprises several practices which are intended to familiarize and ultimately induct the seeker into the Sethian sacramental stream.

It is regarded as one way of accessing the so-called Cabinet, where all further Sethian initiations are given and all work is performed.

There are instructions on how actions are to be performed and how the room is to be decorated. I have put these instructions in italics so that they do not drown in the rest of the text. Where these instructions are vague, I encourage the reader to use his or her artistic capacity, imagining how the work is to be performed.

Acknowledgments

I wish to thank everyone who has helped me preparing this book, and especially members of the Sodalitas Sanctum Seth and the Krystiania publishing team.

The Moricario

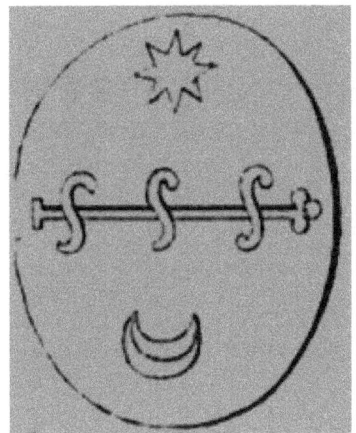

To the Solitary Sethian Seeker

SSS

The Preparations

And Moricario said: "Let this work be performed as in a dream."

The preparations consist of a description of the room, the dressing and the altar used in the Moricario workings. They are guidelines and may differ between sequences due to specific descriptions or the understanding of the art of the practitioner. The mindset of the Solitary Sethian Seeker should be as if he or she was practicing within a lucid dream.

The room

The room should be viewed as a representation of the Seeker's own inner being. It may be a place dedicated to the Sethian work or a room created for the occasion, a space that is created and later disassembled.
Know the significance of your choice before you initiate your work.

The dressing

Let the Solitary Sethian Seeker dress in simple clean black garments as his or her regular working clothes.
The Mask of Art and the Common Black Cloak are worn in the workings after they are retrieved (instructions will follow).

The altar

Let the altar be prepared with a large black cloth, with a white candle in the center, placed on a representation of the Word of Seth (A Sethian book).
Place a veiled representation of Our Lady in the World of Form by the candle, together with a chalice full of rich red wine. The incense used is preferably made of roses. The dagger and the bell will also rest upon the altar when they are retrieved (instructions will follow).

The meditation

When meditating, let the Seeker sit in a chair, hands resting on his lap, spine straight, eyes closed.
Let him recite the word "Sha-rai-wa" continuously in his mind, focusing on its sound and movement without tension or strain. If he is disturbed by thoughts or sleepiness and drifts away from the word, let him continue his recitation as soon as he discovers he has lost it.
When meditating in this manner, there is no good or poor meditation; it is just meditation.
This meditation processes, digests and integrates the experiences and memories of the Seeker to the Sethian stream of transmission. It should be done in this manner every day for an appropriate time on an everyday basis during the work.

Preludium

By the tears and the blood
of the lost and the slain
the Angel of Time
sets the clock and its reign
and the Word became flesh

The stars and the planets
They rose and they set
Their fiery strings
through the fabric of flesh

And the strings and the rings
puppets and bells
they sing and they ring
going 'round and 'round
And the angels were sighing
as the demons were laughing
and the time it was ticking away

From "The Sethian Clock"
The Charaxio (privately published)

The song of Seth

> And when the bell knells once
> The serpent sings
> To his sons and his daughters
> As the Christ appears

Come to me Seth said
Come to me in the name of Man
Come to me at the knell of the bell

And his daughter and son Moricario came
And with Moricario the aeon and the light within
And the coming was a descent
On the stairway of Time
To the Chamber of Flesh

And as Moricario opened his or her mouth
The heavens were strewn with several stars
And the ashes anointed all similar spirits
As the bell continued to knell

Both aeons enshrouded in the cloak
Prepared for the event of Time
Seth unsealed his cloak and his chest
And Horaia retrieved a luminous book

And One consented
And All consented
And Moricario consented
And music was everywhere

As the book was burning
The aeons were praying
Seth was singing
And Horaia embraced the light

And Moricario kneeled
As he entered the book
With his aeon and angels
And the Gate was sealed once again

And the song commenced
Forever in the book
The Word of Seth
In which Moricario partook

The Calling of the Watchers of the Work

> When the bell knells twice
> The Word and the Silence unite
> The One Initiator arises
> As the Christ descends

Before going to sleep, the Seeker approaches the hidden altar of Art, prepared in the usual manner.
Let the Seeker meditate on the flame for a time.
The Seeker will then begin the process of accessing the spiritual chamber of Moricario:

The Blessing of the Light

There is a fire hidden in the depths of the universe,
moving, resting, coming forth, hiding....
O Unknown Father, Great Invisible Spirit,
thy Barbelo embraces us, and thy Autogenes is with us.
Hidden are the mansions of dreams, visions and nightmares;
I call forth the light that illuminates the world.

Invocation of the Watcher of the Work

It is revealed to us by Horaia-A-Zoarazo:
"Blessed are you, where you are, I will be with you.
Call for me and I will be with you, for I am in you, as you are in me.

Blessed are you who hear the sound of my voice in all that is as the hoarse hissing voice of the burning embers on dark and lonely autumn nights.
Call for me, and I will be the hidden door at the threshold of time".
By the force of the Fullness, hidden in the fallen world,
I call you!
By the blood and the water, the rivers of my veins,
I call you as you have taught us to call!
I call you to open the work of the Sethian path.
I call you to send me the Watcher and guide of this sacred path, revealed to your faithful Master Amarantus, in a moment long past, when he was Amarant-tra-Zorai.

I call for the presence of Mori-zorai, Lady of the angels of Safir, Watcher of the movement of Metanoi in Man. Mistress of Mirrors and weaver of the Path.
Mori-zorai Mori-zorai
Mori-zorai Mori-zorai
Mori-zorai Mori-zorai

Parting of the Curtains

Let it be according to the Words of Seth,
Let the work begin and the Mystery unfold before my Life.
Let the liquid key open the lock
Of dreaming eyes
Through realms of silent song
Through visions lost in grief and sleep
To the journey of the one and the none
The pilgrim of the night
The pilgrim of the light
This son/daughter of the serpentine Sophia
reunited in One.

Unveil the representation of Our Lady in the world of form.

The Liquid Key

The Seeker addresses the wine with hands hovering over the chalice.

Only as one may this path be opened and won.
Only as one may the lock be revealed and undone.
Only through this wine may the boundaries be gone
In the Name of Seth-Hor-I.

The Seeker anoints the representation of Our Lady and his or her heart with drops of wine.
The Seeker then kisses the rim of the chalice and says:

Through this wine
(*name*) and Mori-zorai
are One in the work of the Sethian path, the fulfillment of the Moricario.

Drinks the wine in one take.
Places it upside down on the altar, and says:

It is done; it has begun!

Retrieving the Tools

> When the bell knells thrice
> The crossroads flow forth
> From the lips of the Wise
> As the Christ walks the earth

Retrieving a tool is easy, however it is not the tool in itself we seek, it is the symbolic reality hidden in its artistic nature. Having truly retrieved a tool means to have received it on a physical, mental and spiritual level, and gained the insight that there is really no difference between these so called levels of perception. The general preparations for this work have always been dictated by the Spirit of the Art in accordance with the Solitary Sethian Seeker.

The Mask of Art

Let it be remembered that after Cain, the son of Nebroel had killed Abel the son of Yaldabout, Man and Woman conjoined with each other. This first carnal unification gave birth to the first born man of Man. And into this house of flesh, Seth descended from his meditation within the fullness of being. Thus the Man of Light was incarnate in the world of form.
It is by remembrance of this act that the mystery of true self-knowledge came to be.
This act is remembered and understood by the Mask of Art.

The Mask of Art must be created by the hands of the Seeker. Make it of plaster and bandages in the fashion of a half-mask.
When the white mask is prepared, let the seeker meditate in darkness contemplating his or her dim reflection in a mirror. The only light is a stick of incense placed before the mirror. The contemplation lasts until the incense is burned down. During the work the Seeker continuously repeats the following sentence with a low voice:
"Metanoi Metanoi Metanoi, reveal my faceless face".

The impression made by this contemplation is to be painted on the mask. This is the persona of the Seeker in all Sethian work, except where otherwise prescribed. Thus the Mask of Art is retrieved from oblivion.

The Common Black Cloak

Let it be remembered that to render himself unknown to the world, Seth wore the black cloak of the pilgrim, and as a stranger he went to the men of the Forest of Forgetfulness.
Invisible to the forces of the Creator and the Opposer he wanders the realms of existence as water on rocks and dust in the wind.
And the cloak was tailored as customs prescribed, revealing neither riches nor poverty to the eye in the sky.
This act is remembered and understood by the Common Black Cloak.

To retrieve the Common Black Cloak the Seeker must be able to locate a used black cloak or create a new cloak of used black fabric. It is to "reveal neither riches nor poverty".
Let the Seeker perform one or more pilgrimages to a desolate place of some significance and meditate as described previously, wearing the cloak. The period of meditation is done when the cloak has become the Seeker's secret skin. Thus the Common Black Cloak is retrieved from oblivion.

The Dagger Zora-Arthor

Let it be remembered that when Seth walks the earth, he is the master of masks and an eternal High Priest. The Rose Blood of his heart is full of Love for the redemption of the Children. Therefore his heart is crowned with a serpent. So do not expect rest in his presence, for his Love knows no mercy. And as Zorakatora he brought a blade to his people so that they would not travel in darkness unarmed.

This act is remembered and understood by the dagger called Zora-Arthor or just Arthora.

To retrieve the dagger the Seeker must be freely given a dagger from an unknown. This is by its own right a test of cunning. The dagger will have a black hilt, or be painted black upon receiving it.

Know that whoever gives it to you is, during the act, under the influence of Zorakatora. Thus the Dagger, Arthora, is retrieved from oblivion.

The Sethian Clock

Let it be remembered that the beginning and the end are at the turning of the ring. It is all in the Fullness. The Sethian clock is a singing brass bell. It is the herald of movement and rest and its secret unlocks the sanctuary, even Mount Charaxio, as Seth himself meditated there with his clock.
This act is remembered and understood by the Sethian Clock.

To retrieve the brass bell called the Sethian Clock, the Seeker must find a bell crafted in the mountains. The Sethian seeker will then practice with the bell, making a regular rhythmic sound until it enables him to enter the trance of lucid dream. Thus the Sethian Clock is retrieved from oblivion.

The Dedication

> When the bell knells five
> I, the rebus of Gnosis
> Fullness enshrouded by flesh, thrive
> As the Christ is alive

Let the Solitary Sethian Seeker meditate at the edge of a river on a starless night. Let him know himself, when in the world, to be of the same nature as the river. When this knowledge is firmly attained, he puts his left hand on his heart and speaks to the river:

Run river run, for everything turns
I am firm and I am flexible
Ever changing remaining the same
A pilgrim am I to the turning of the time

He then put his right hand into the moving water and speaks to the water:

I enter you as you have entered me,
And I call the Master of the prophet-priest to hear me
Zorakatora, master of sacraments and hearer of oaths.
I call you to listen as I gaze at the face of the River of Time

Zorakatora harai a Zorai
Zorakatora harai a Zorai
Zorakatora harai a Zorai
Zorakatora harai a Zorai
Zorakatora harai a Zorai

He then puts both hands on his heart.

Through journey and wit I have reclaimed my tools
Now to be blessed I dedicate myself:
I will seek my fulfillment by the Sethian word, by the voice of the Mountain and the Serpent and the Dove.

He then plunges the bell and the dagger into the river. He draws them forth and anoints the mask and the cloak with the tip of the dagger, dripping with water, as he slowly sounds the bell several times.

It is done, a fullness completed and a new one begun.

The Epiphany

> When the bell knells six
> The aeon and illusion
> Flash back and forth as they mix
> As the Christ walks the earth

This rite is a self-initiation, it is the answer to the Dedication, inviting the Solitary Sethian Seeker to receive a blessing to the extent of his or her capacity.

Let the Solitary Sethian Seeker prepare himself or herself by meditating on the Letters of Adamas. One letter each day; the same letter each morning and evening.

When this is done, prepare a scented bath with the following herbs: Cinnamon, sandalwood and rose, and add a glass of white wine. Keep the water alive and running.

Let the room be illuminated with several candles, and incense of the same herbs as those in the bath.

Prepare the chalice by filling it with red wine and place it on the altar. Strike the bell 8 times over the water.

The Prayer of Eleleth

O Unknown Father, Great Invisible Spirit,
thy Barbelo embraces us, and thy Autogenes is with us.
Hidden are the mansions of dreams, visions and nightmares;
I call forth the light that illuminates the world.
O Eleleth; true Light, Light that dissolves the darkness
of the heavenly velvet night;
force that pulls the veil aside
for those who live in the kingdom of the warring forces.
You are the Light that glows, warms, devours.
We see you and recognize you
as Eleleth in the Four Luminaries;
O luminous angel of peacock feathers
and dove's winter plumage;
the guide from the Fullness in this Abode of Night.

Shuffle your deck of Adamas cards, and draw 4.
Read the verses of the 4 cards in the order you drew them as a single poem. Read to Eleleth, Moricario and the water.
Use the dagger to engrave the 4 letters on the face of the water, as you sing their names several times.
Enter the water and visualize your union with the forces invoked.
As this is accomplished, invoke Sethorai to bless you.

In the name of the Invisible Spirit and the luminous water.
Come Sethorai, my light restored and fullness revealed.
By the path of the lightning, moving hither and thither,
By the hand of the Initiator and his Word,
and to our Lady of Light,
Let your light descend to this water and wine
Let me meet I, One and None at the crossroads of time.

Rise from the bath, drape yourself in the cloak, walk to the altar, anoint the chalice with water and drink all the wine.
The Solitary Sethian Seeker then continues to chant the following for as long as deemed fit:

Sethorai-Morika-Metanoi-IAO

When it is fulfilled, withdraw in silent meditation.

The Vision of the Cross

> When the bell knells four
> The conclaves are shut
> The lamps are lit by our luminous lore
> As the Christ walks the earth

Bring to your secret sanctuary the dagger and a single red rose, together with the chalice and flasks of dark and bright wine. Arrange these components on your altar and be seated before them in silent meditation.
Summon then, before your inner eye, the following sequence of images and events:

Experience your individuality as surrounded by the eternal fullness, in perfect peace and perfect balance. Allow yourself merge with this eternity.
Let the scenery then divide into an eternity of white and an eternity of black, as limitless curtains meeting before your eyes. Know that these curtains are made of the substances contained in your two flasks.
Feel how they define each other, how they balance without uniting.

See your dagger slowly pierce through the curtains. Watch how the fullness bleeds through the texture. As it seeps through, it formulates the 'In-Between' which coagulates into the Sethian cross.

As the fullness continues to pulse through the light and the dark colors, it reaches the altar at the foundation of All. There the blood collects in the middle of the chalice in the form of a rose. For each drop the Sethian Clock sounds in your mind.
When you raise your inner eye, you become aware that the cross is gone from the curtains, it is all in the chalice.
 Gazing a second time into the chalice see the rose transform into a man; realize that the blood is truly your own.

When you have meditated on the substance in the chalice, continue with your eyes half-opened.
Put your hands upon the empty chalice and whisper:

Sacrament of One and of None, it is already fulfilled.

Pour the content of the two flasks into the chalice simultaneously and whisper:

Broken circle, Clock and Cloak, life or death, the road to the Sphinx and the mysterious One.

Take the dagger in your left hand.
Pierce the wine in the middle of the chalice with the dagger and whisper:

Thus is the first act of those who will walk the path that is not a path.

Take the rose, which is holy to Our Lady, in your right hand and prick your thumb on a thorn. Let a drop of blood enter the wine.

Thus is the second act of those who will knock at the door flowing in the air.

Visualize the Sethian cross in the wine, and say:

And thus are all the acts of those who will enter.

Drink all the wine, and say:

To view the world from in-between.

The Seeker kisses the rose and rests it on the rim of the chalice.

And as Aberamento I also speak:
"Always for the sake of Love.
Always for the sake of Redemption.
Always for the sake of the Mystery.
And always, always for the sake of Man.
Always for the sake of Her".
Yes, always for the sake of Her!

The Cloak of Seth

> When the bell knells seven
> The stars and the planets are fading
> They hide in their mansions of heaven
> As the Christ walks the earth

This is the rite of disappearing within the present.

The realities of the Archons, are only true when men and women move into memories of the past, or hopes, desires or fears for the future. Meditation anchored in the present, without any evaluations of past or present and no thoughts for the future, turns the Sethian invisible to the Archons as they themselves become One. This is a daily practice for the accomplished Sethians of the Amarantian school.

The Sethian practitioner is seated, prepared for meditation.
The Sethian is enfolded in the cloak, lights an incense stick and meditates no more than the duration of its burning.

The practice is introduced by the Ver-Quon Chamoth.

Ver-Quon Chamoth

Two paths:
choose none.
Lightning and Truth
cannot be resisted
when they strike
All
Many
One
None
One
Many
All

Equilibrium is not
a frozen state
but indifferent movement
between extremities.

The Sethian then meditates.
To conclude the practice, the Sethian breathes deeply five times and internalizes the cloak and enters the eternal Present.

Intermezzo

In slumber waiting for the present to become now
Sleeping, preparing for the future
Awake, dreaming of the past

Thus life was chased into death
And death into life

Break the boundary
And death dies in every moment
Whenever entering the fleeting present

Ever stepping into the gate of existence

A torch to heaven and a carafe of water to hell

The Litany of Adamas

> When the bell knells eight
> The vaults in the skies are shut
> By the hand of the feathery angel of fate
> As the Christ walks the earth

The Seeker approaches the hidden altar of Art, prepared in the usual manner. Wine is poured into the chalice. All letters of Adamas are present. The Clock is sounded between each verse.

Adamas invincible power.
Adamas Logos, Invisible Spirit:
Everything is your emanation
Everything an ebb and a flow
Leaving for nowhere
Ever returning

In between One, Autogenes
And the triple realm:
Father – Mother – Son,
true reality: ORA MOR RA TRO MORICARIO.
All, Many, One, None, Open!

IEN IEN EA EA EA ADAMAS

Adamas, light radiating from the light,
eye of the light, first man,
annulling deficiency.

IEN IEN EA EA EA ADAMAS

Adamas,
perfect man,
eye of Autogenes
Unite.

IEN IEN EA EA EA
IEN IEN EA EA EA
IEN IEN EA EA EA

Boundless Nature
cannot descend
And when it does
will rise again
AION IEN IEN EA EA EA ADAMAS

The Unknown Master
makes masks
from Mirrors
Thinks Truth
from Tales
weaves Worlds
from words
HELI IEN IEN EA EA EA ADAMAS

If the Sleeper Awakens,
If the Vessel is broken
even death
will die
RASH IEN IEN EA EA EA ADAMAS

The Dead God
sleeps in the husk of his body
The Living God
moves through the universe
in the Vessel of his Mystery
ZOTH IEN IEN EA EA EA ADAMAS

When the Beginning
consumes
the End,
the Instant
becomes perpetual death
and infinite resurrection
MOR IEN IEN EA EA EA ADAMAS

When time turns cold
and the chains change creed:
When you break against
the unmoving point,
The All will revolve around One:
and One will attain unto None
PHILON IEN IEN EA EA EA ADAMAS

ADAMAS ADAMAS ADAMAS
AION IEN IEN EA EA EA ADAMAS
HELI IEN IEN EA EA EA ADAMAS
RASH IEN IEN EA EA EA ADAMAS
ZOTH IEN IEN EA EA EA ADAMAS
MOR IEN IEN EA EA EA ADAMAS
PHILON IEN IEN EA EA EA ADAMAS
ADAMAS ADAMAS ADAMAS

Father – Mother – Son,
true reality: ORA MOR RA TRO MORICARIO.
All, Many, One, None, Open!

IEN IEN EA EA EA ADAMAS

I, Adamas, light radiating from the light,
I, eye of the light, first man,
I am united.

IEN IEN EA EA EA ADAMAS

Adamas, Sethoraia
Perfect Man,
Eye, Breath, Flesh:
Unite.

Drink the wine in the chalice.

By IEN IEN EA EA EA ADAMAS
It is done!
It is fulfilled.

The Rite of the Self-born

> When the bell knells nine
> The quick and the dead are fulfilled
> And Horaia-Hor-Ai touches the veins of the wine
> As the Christ walks the earth

Before going to sleep, the Sethian approaches the hidden altar of Art, prepared in the usual manner.
Light the Candle and the incense and say:

Great Invisible Spirit
Father, Mother, Son
IAO-OIA-EUI
Come Seth, come father of our kin.
Come Self-born father of all the self-born ones.
Life is lived in death, but death does not see it.
Love blesses Man, but Man does not receive it.
Come O I and You united; Light of Man.
Come O I and You united; Light bearer, Fallen, Redeemer.
Come O I and You united; Chameleon-Christ and the Phoenix-angel's egg.
And I am as I always was, a Heart Encircled by a Serpent; Come Forth and Follow.

The Sethian strikes the Clock thrice with the dagger and touches the representation of the word of Seth with his hand then points the tip of the dagger towards his hand.

First, the sacraments are revealed; hidden from the generations.
Then the Priest-prophets return.
Then the doctrine returns.
Then the Children awake; at the magical union.
Such are Our words!

Strikes thirteen knells.

He then touches the wine with the tip of the dagger and says:

Only as one may this path be opened and won.
Only as none may the Mystery be real and become.
Only through this wine may the boundaries be undone
In the Name of Seth-Hor-I.

The Sethian anoints the representation of Our Lady with wine.

Ancient ancestor and eternal Now, Seth, the first Man in the eternity of the Fullness.
You are the moving reality of the Origin.
You are the Son of Barbelo and the anointed Autogenes.
You are crowned with the Four Luminaries, and you are the beginning and end.
You are the Master of Life, Light and luminous Love which are the conditions for realizing the Mystery.
O Father of Life, one with the Father, one with your kin.
Let me participate in you, as I have entered Moricario.

He then marks his chest with the Sethian cross and continues:

I have taken up my cross, your cross, our cross. The sign of the present and ever-being, the sign of the Self-born. I partake in and through Moricario. As I seek induction into the life of the Mountain.

He then drinks the wine.

One God, One Man, and One Infinite Existence. Amen.

He meditates for as long as he see fit, then snuffs the candle.

The Blessing of the River

> When the bell knells ten
> The chalice is filled once again
> And the Initiator smiles
> As the Christ ascends

So prepare your heart, but harden it not, for that which is hardened will burst. Only the one who remains like a river or a serpent, will heed my call.
The ways of the world and old age harden those who are asleep, but these are not of us, and will remain in the circle. Partake, and become the flow.

I am the first and the last.
Discovering the Mystery
at the end of the circle
changing yet ever One, Child of the River.

I am honored and reviled.
Wearing the mask
of all humankind
changing yet ever One, Child of the River.

I am the solace of my pain and pleasure.
I have created them all in my Mind
and I behold them as a dream
changing yet ever One, Child of the River.

I am the bride and the groom.
United
for the sake of Love
moving revolving and coming forth.

I am the incomprehensible silence and the diversity of thought.
The point and the circle
reality unreal
moving revolving and coming forth.

I am the voice whose sound is manifold.
Carrying the Sethian song
singing creation and destruction
moving revolving and coming forth.

I am godless, and I have a great God.
This Logos
has yet spoken my existence.
And the water and I are One.

I am unification and resolution.
Breaking through the texture of reality
I am Light come forth in the present
And the water and I are One.

I am who I am, persistent and resolute.
Descended into the river
I ascend the sacred mountain
and enter the Cabinet.

The Secret Seal

When the bell knells eleven
The Snake and the Dove reveal the hidden redemption
The Initiator smiles
And the Christ ascends

If the light of Moricario is revealed, the Sethian may mark himself with a secret sign or tattoo, the Sethian cross or a suitable hidden ornament.

If the Sethian wishes to honor this custom he will put his hand on the tattoo and visualize the Sethian path leading In-Between. Uniting with the moment he reads the following text as he sees the scene vividly:

And the Sethian Master Aboron said:
The rivers of wine, they were flowing.
And the angel turned and he turned and he turned, in circles of creation and destruction at the borders and gateways of reality, unfulfilled.
The Maskmaker's quill was dipped in his blood and the line there drawn was the mask of the master to come. And the walls of the chapel and the blood of the quill wield the magic of Voices, of forces and faces; fading forever in time.
And the rivers of wine they were flowing and flowing
To the beginning of the ending of now.

Thus ends the practice.

It is done, it is done, it is done. Moricario, Sethorai, Alpha Omega. It is Done!

Postludium

I have spoken, said Moricario
The path is revealed, yet few will follow
as the true traveler will lose all in order to gain all
and the Mystery will wash them away
and all that remains will be the new born Artist,
Raising his eyes to the Mountain.

Veni Sethorai

> When the bell knells twelve
> The Word is fulfilled
> The Initiated smiles
> As the Christ ascends

Come, Sethorai, Rose-blooded blest,
and in our hearts take up Thy rest;
let the Light of the Fullness descend,
To fill the hearts here to ascend.

O Lightbringer, to Thee we cry,
Thou divine Life of Light most high,
Thou Fount of Life, and Fire of Love,
and sweet Lightwater from above.

O Presence of the Mind divine,
the divine gift of Gnostic truths are thine;
true Logos of the Father thou,
who dost the tongue with power endow.

Thy Life to every sense impart,
and shed thy Light in every heart;
together One divinity
divested of all infirmity.

Drive far away the Ruler's woe,
and thine abiding peace bestow;
if thou be our luminous guide,
no folly can our steps betide.

Praise we the Unknown and His Son
and Holy Spirit, all are One;
and that the Son on us bestows
the Gnosis that from Fullness flows.

The Work of the Cabinet

> When the bell knells thirteen
> The echo is Silent
> the light shines in the darkness
> darkness comprehending it not.

Before going to sleep, the Seeker approaches the hidden altar of Art in darkness.
The bell is sounded thirteen times.

Opening the Cabinet

The Prayer of Eleleth

The flame is lit.

O Unknown Father, Great Invisible Spirit,
thy Barbelo embraces us, and thy Autogenes is with us.
Hidden are the mansions of dreams, visions andnightmares;
I call forth the light that illuminates the world.
O Eleleth; true Light, Light that dissolves the darkness
of the heavenly velvet night;
force that pulls the veil aside
for those who live in the kingdom of the warring forces.
You are the Light that glows, warms, devours.
We see you and recognize you
as Eleleth in the Four Luminaries;
O luminous angel of peacock feathers
and dove's winter plumage;
the guide from the Fullness in this Abode of Night.

The Blessing of the Light

Light the incense.

There is a fire hidden in the depths of the universe,
moving, resting, coming forth, hiding.
O Unknown Father, Great Invisible Spirit,
thy Barbelo embraces us, and thy Autogenes is with us.
Hidden are the mansions of dreams, visions and nightmares;
I call forth the light that illuminates the world,
to bless and sanctify our work.
Invocation of the Watcher of the Work

It is revealed to us by Horaia-A-Zoarazo
"Blessed are you, where you are, I will be with you.
Call for me and I will be with you, for I am in you, as you are in me.
Blessed are you who hear the sound of my voice in all that is, as the hoarse hissing voice of the burning embers on dark and lonely autumn nights.
Call for me and I will be the hidden door at the threshold of time".
By the force of the Fullness, hidden in the fallen world,
I call you!
By the blood and the water, the rivers of my veins,
I call you as you have asked me to call!
I call you, to open the work of the Sethian path.
I call you to send to me the Watcher and guide of this sacred path, revealed to your faithful Master Amarantus, when he was Amarant-tra-Zorai.

I call for the presence of Mori-zorai, Lady of the angels of Safir, Watcher of the movement of Metanoi in Man. Mistress of Mirrors and weaver of the Path.

Parting of the Curtains

Let it be according to the Words of Seth,
Let the work begin and the Mystery unfold before my Life.
Let the liquid key open the lock
Of dreaming eyes
Through realms of silent song
Through visions lost in grief and sleep
To the journey of the one and the none
The pilgrim of the night
The pilgrim of the light
This son/daughter of the serpentine Sophia
reunited in One.

Unveil the representation of Our Lady in the world of form.

Two Sacraments

The Sacrament of the Present

In slumber waiting for the present to become now
Sleeping, preparing for the future
Awake, dreaming of the past

Thus life was chased into death
And death into life

Break the boundary
And death dies in every moment
Whenever entering the persistent present

Ever stepping into the gate of existence

A torch to heaven and a bucket of water to hell

Meditate for half an hour.

The Sacrament of the Kin

Touch the secret seal and connect to yourself.

And the Sethian Master Aboron said:
The rivers of wine, they were flowing.
And the angel turned and he turned and he turned, in circles of creation and destruction at the borders and gateways of reality, unfulfilled.
The Maskmaker's quill was dipped in his blood and the line there drawn was the mask of the master to come. And the walls of the chapel and the blood of the quill, wield the magic of Voices, of forces and faces; fading forever in time.
And the rivers of wine they were flowing and flowing
To the beginning of the ending of now.

Put your hands upon the empty chalice and whisper:

Sacrament of One and of None, it is already fulfilled.

Pour wine into the chalice as you say:

The river ran from the sacred mountain.

Whisper to the chalice:

Broken circle, Clock and Cloak, life and death, the road to the Sphinx and the mysterious One.

Take the dagger in your left hand.
Pierce the wine in the middle of the chalice with the dagger and whisper:

Thus is the first act of the pilgrim of the path that is not a path

Wave the rose incense over the chalice.

Thus is the second act of knocking at Reality, of One and of None.

Visualize the Sethian cross in the wine and say:

And thus are all the acts of those who enter the One and the None.

Drink all the wine.

To view the world from In-between.
The past and the future.
Thus I receive what is.

The Seeker kisses the statue and veils her once more.

Closing the Cabinet

Come, Sethorai, Rose-blooded blest,
and in our hearts take up Thy rest;
let the Light of the Fullness descend,
To fill the hearts here to ascend.

O Lightbringer, to Thee we cry,
Thou divine Life of Light most high,
Thou Fount of Life, and Fire of Love,
and sweet Lightwater from above.

O Presence of the Mind divine,
the divine gift of Gnostic truths are thine;
true Logos of the Father thou,
who dost the tongue with power endow.

Thy Life to every sense impart,
and shed thy Light in every heart;
together One divinity
divesting all infirmity.

The bell is sounded thirteen times and the lights are snuffed.

The Amarantian Sethian School

Fin de "Gnostica del Arte"

Appendix

The Book of Adamas

"Adamas asked for a son, so that his offspring might father the incorruptible race. Our Mother opened herself for him, and shed her blood into his dream. And through his son, the silence and the voice appeared. When this came to pass, through him, that which was dead rose itself and dissolved. This is the Book of Adamas: the twenty two drops of blood that the Mother shed into his dream, so that Seth might restore and destroy that which is, and is not. Those who draw them, grasp them and dream them will find the unwritten keys to open themselves: They are mirrors, not of the soul, but of the spirit."

AION

Boundless Nature
cannot descend
And when it does
will rise again

BEÏN

I am the Light
shining in the Darkness:
And the Darkness
Shines in the Vessel
As Silence comprehendeth me
not

GOMOR

I am the Self-Begotten:
untouched, undying
Unfolding the
Vastness
of my Being

DÏN

I am the Absolute:
Unrelenting Truth
unconditional Being
continual Movement
and unbridled Beauty

HELI

The Unknown Master
makes masks
from Mirrors
Thinks Truth
from Tales
weaves Worlds
from words

VR

Two paths:
chose none.
Lightning and Truth
cannot be resisted
when they strike

ZOTH

The Dead God
sleeps in the husk of his body

The Living God
moves through the universe
in the Vessel of his Mystery

CHAMOTH

Equilibrium is not
a frozen state
but indifferent movement
between extremities

THELI

The Light-Seed coils
in the spine of the word,
under the cloak of matter,
springs forth
from silence
into ecstasy

IA

Man is a riddle whose answer is Truth
Dare to Ask
Will to Seek
Know to Knock
And keep Silent
of what is opened unto you

CATH

Art
is Desire
directed
by Will

LUZ

Sacrifice
is forsaking
what you love
and those
who love you

MOR

When the Beginning
consumes
the End,
the Instant
becomes perpetual death
and infinite resurrection

NAÏN

There are two waters
Of Heavenly Bliss
and Infernal Frenzy
And the Waters are One

XÏRON

There is a Patcher
of patterns
and pictures
With seams and stiches
binding beings together
under layers
of lies

OYN

There is a gate
into the heights of hell
into the depths of heaven
through the mirror:
Enter

PHILON

When time turns cold
and the chains change creed:
When you break against
the unmoving point,
The All will revolve around One:
and One will attain unto None

TSÏD

When darkness mixes with light
a neither-or is born

QUON

All

Many

One

All   Many   One   None   One   Many   All

One

Many

All

RASH

If the Sleeper Awakens,
If the Vessel is broken
even death
will die

SETH

The Uncreated Light
contains the world
breaks the egg
consumes Heaven
extinguishes Hell

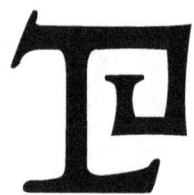

THUM

The Broken World
is a White bone Prison
a broken mirror
a cloak of smoke
a veil of words
shattering all
whom enter

KRYSTIANIA PUBLICATIONS:

Ødegaard, Rune: Nøkkelen: Sethiansk gnostisisme i praksis 2009

Svela, Ove Joachim: Kabbalah: Vestens levende mysterietradisjon 2010

Ødegaard, Rune: Corpus Hermeticum 2010

Ødegaard Rune: Salomos Oder 2011

Ødegaard, Rune: The Key: Sethian Gnosticism in the postmodern world 2011

Ødegaard, Rune: The Gate: Sethian Gnosticism in the postmodern world 2012

Nykland, Sølvi: Noreas Bok: Drømmer om døden og skapelse 2013

de la Croix, Désir: Martinistordenen Ordre Reaux Croix 2013

Ødegaard, Rune: Veien er Zen: Bodhidharmas lære 2013

Ødegaard, Rune: Porten: Sethiansk gnostisisme i praksis 2013

Evjen, Knut: Teofobi: Den gudfryktiges åpenbaring 2013

Ødegaard, Rune & Lindalen, Turi: Frostfjell: Zen-poesi fra fjellet 2013

www.ingramcontent.com/pod-product-compliance
Lightning Source LLC
Chambersburg PA
CBHW030359100426
42812CB00028B/2774/J